WOMEN OF THE HOME FRONT

WOMEN OF THE HOME FRONT

SERVING THE NATION IN PHOTOGRAPHS

INTRODUCTION BY ELISABETH SHIPTON

All images are provided by Mirrorpix and are available to purchase from
www.vintagephotosonline.co.uk

First published 2019

The History Press
97 George's Place,
Cheltenham, Gloucestershire, GL50 3QB
www.thehistorypress.co.uk

British Library Cataloguing in Publication Data.
A catalogue record for this book is available from the British Library.

ISBN 978 0 7509 9073 8

Typesetting and origination by The History Press
Printed in Turkey by Imak

CONTENTS

INTRODUCTION

'Women of Britain – Come Forward Now!'

'You are being asked to volunteer at once ...'

'We Need the Women – What About You?'

Towards the end of the 1930s, war in Europe seemed inevitable and Britain began to prepare. This time its population would be on the front line and mass mobilisation would be needed on an unprecedented scale. Women would have to take on new civilian roles and join the armed forces, releasing men to fight. The sight of women in uniform, working on farms and on public transport was at first a novelty attracting interested spectators, but as the war went on their number grew and they became more generally accepted. By 1944 over 7 million women were engaged in war work with over 640,000 in the armed forces and more than 80,000 in the Women's Land Army. These women played a significant role in supporting the war effort and keeping the country running.

Britain had employed women's auxiliary services in the First World War, but this only began after two and a half years of conflict when facing a severe shortage of manpower. The Women's Army Auxiliary Corps, the Women's Royal Naval Service and the Women's Royal Air Force were all disbanded by 1921. As war approached again there were increasing calls from ex-servicewomen and enlightened members of the different military branches for the services to be reinstated, this time before the conflict started.

First to be established was the Auxiliary Territorial Service (ATS) in September 1938, supporting the army, followed by the Women's Royal Naval Service (WRNS) in April 1939 and then the Women's Auxiliary Air Force (WAAF) in June 1939. Alongside these, the Women's Land Army – another First World War organisation – was re-established in June 1939–50, to provide agricultural workers.

To begin with the three auxiliary military services recruited women on a voluntary basis, to undertake basic domestic and clerical jobs, and typically selecting those already doing similar work in civilian life. This meant they only required minimal training and could be deployed relatively quickly. The first ATS recruits became clerks, cooks, store women, drivers and orderlies (cleaners). Domestic work was not particularly popular, though, and for those who did join up it usually meant taking a pay cut, as servicewomen were generally paid about two-thirds the amount that men doing the same job received. Yet, the women were given uniforms (saving valuable clothing coupons), plus food and accommodation if they were stationed away from home.

The Second World War began for Britain on 3 September 1939 and immediately volunteers were called for. Those women under the age of 21 needed their parents' permission to enrol in the auxiliary services. Mothers and fathers were reluctant and needed persuading. They were concerned about accusations of impropriety against their daughters because they would be working alongside men, often in remote locations away from home. However, over the course of the war the situation began to change. Fathers joined the Home Guard and their daughters argued it was only fair that they could take on war work too. The impact of bombing raids, the loss of life and damage to their home towns, made the British public determined to do what they could to stand up to the aggressor.

Within two years, the women's auxiliary services became more organised, dramatically increasing the different roles undertaken and providing the necessary training. The ATS operated anti-aircraft batteries, stopping short of firing on the enemy (women being active combatants was seen as a step too far); the WRNS trained its members in communications and mechanics; and the WAAF employed radar operators and meteorologists, to name just a few.

The majority of women volunteers worked in the civilian sector, as drivers and conductors on public transport, in factories that produced munitions and in dockyards building ships. By December 1943, one in three factory workers was female and there was also a significant increase in children's nurseries to allow mothers to work.

In contrast to work in factories and administrative or domestic roles in the auxiliaries, the Women's Land Army offered a 'healthy open-air life', but it was physically demanding, involved handling heavy farm machinery and the hours were long. Before the war, Britain had imported the majority of its food; now in wartime it had to be self-sufficient. Women undertook animal and dairy farming for much-needed food, as well as producing fruit and vegetables, and flax growing produced linen swhich was hugely valuable during the wartime clothes shortage.

More female workers were needed and, as volunteers could leave at any time, the British Government took decisive action. In December 1941, Britain introduced the conscription of all unmarried women and childless widows aged 20–30. Those called up were given the choice of joining one of the three auxiliary services: the Women's Land Army, civil defence or working in industry.

Demobilisation of the auxiliary services began in 1945 after Victory in Europe (VE) Day on 8 May 1945, and the Second World War officially ended on 2 September 1945. As the wartime economy transitioned back to peacetime, factories were closed or reverted back to their pre-war use and the number of jobs available for women was dramatically reduced. As men returned home, they went back to their old jobs and, in 1950, the Women's Land Army was disbanded.

Yet the three women's auxiliary services were not disbanded. Instead, in 1948 the Army and Air Force (Women's Service) Act was passed, creating a permanent peacetime role for women in Britain's armed forces. On 1 February 1949 the ATS was succeeded by the Women's Royal Army Corps, the WRNS kept its title and the WAAF became the Women's Royal Air Force once more. The roles available to women were scaled back from wartime, once more focusing on domestic and clerical jobs. In the decades that followed, servicewomen were given more roles and new opportunities. Eventually, by 1994, all three services were integrated into the three main branches of the British Armed Forces.

On 25 October 2018, nearly eighty years after women's auxiliary services were re-established on the eve of the Second World War, Defence Secretary Gavin Williamson announced that all roles in the military were now open to women.

Elisabeth Shipton

1

AUXILIARY TERRITORIAL SERVICE (ATS)

New recruits looking for excitement and adventure may have had a rude awakening when they arrived for training. Typically, they were accommodated in Nissen huts and had to use a communal toilet block. The women had no baths or showers and had to wash alongside one another using hand basins.

Once they had completed their training, the women went to their new posts. A big step forward came in 1941 when they were permitted to work on anti-aircraft batteries for the first time. This was the closest they could get to front-line duty, and by 1942 more women were working on batteries than men. The ATS were also deployed as searchlight operators, tasked with lighting up enemy aircraft so that they could be shot down. The lights also acted as beacons to help RAF aeroplanes to return home.

The membership of the ATS was at its greatest in June 1943, with 214,420 members.

▲ New ATS recruits at the Cowshot Manor Camp, Brookwood, parading before an inspection by Sir Malcolm Fraser and Lord Ashcombe in August 1939.

▲ A new anklet was issued to ATS anti-aircraft (AA) recruits to protect them from early morning dews. Here a line of women lace up their boots in May 1942.

▲ Members of the ATS adjust their caps before a parade, March 1944.

▲ ATS recruits of a mixed heavy AA gun site at Prestwich near Manchester share general duties with the men. Women who have done their spell of day-guard picket being relieved by the men who are going on night guard, April 1942.

◄ Members of the ATS band marching in 1941.

▲ Maldon (Essex) General Training Corps (GTC) Company girls are fast becoming crack rifle shots. Maldon Ladies' Rifle Club have taken them under their wing and are allowing them to use the guns and range. This is part of their training besides the usual GTC training. They are practising sightings with the company looking on and Commandant Samuel teaching, March 1944.

◄ An ATS woman at Western Command ordnance factory undertaking precision work in the instrument department where hundreds of binoculars are turned out, November 1942.

▲ An ATS woman of an east-coast experimental station working at the plotting windows in March 1941. All women working here are specialists and hold degrees.

▲ Girls of the GTC learn Morse code by tapping their fingers on the back of their hand to get them into the rhythm and weight of the tapping before they go on to the Morse keys. The girls in this class at Waddon, Croydon, are busy with their hands learning Morse alphabet in May 1942.

▲ This aeroplane comes apart and can be fitted back together; it is part of the training for the spotters. Here it is being used in October 1943.

▲ Pictures taken at the Royal Army Ordnance Corps (RAOC) depot outside London, in which some of the first ATS volunteers take instruction on rifle shooting at practice camp. A regimental sergeant major is seen demonstrating moving to a position in June 1942.

◄ An ATS operator guiding a searchlight in March 1943. This British Army woman wears the uniform of coat, helmet and earphones.

▲ Just like the real thing, but it's only an exercise, July 1944. ATS women from units in the South West attend Army Fire Control instruction training in bombed Plymouth houses. They learn how to remove casualties from the wreckage and the manual job of clearing away the debris with pick and shovel so they can get at the trapped victims.

➤ A woman of the first ATS Regimental Police Unit at an ATS training centre in the South Eastern Command on 4 October 1941. The women undertake police duties at the gates and are assigned traffic patrol duty.

▲ The first of six ATS recruits who have been chosen to train as Britain's first ace women to use the searchlight, May 1942.

▲ Women from various sections of the ATS collecting spent shells at an experimental establishment of the Ministry of Supply in 1942.

▲ ATS women take part in a tug-of-war competition, August 1941.

◄ A member of the ATS shines her shoes before parade in September 1944.

WOMEN OF THE HOME FRONT

▲ Who pinched the lorry? ATS woman at Western Command ordnance factory rolling out tyres for army trucks in October 1942. Every bit of rubber helps the war effort.

◄ Miss Edith Care, of Evesham, photographed at ATS Western Command ordnance factory in November 1942.

◄ A spoonful of sugar helps the medicine go down: ATS girls seen here taking cod liver oil in March 1941.

◄ The ATS have their own 'Hospital Blues': attractive battledress-style blouses and skirts in blue flannel serge. The first of the uniforms are being worn at Chestis Military Hospital in October 1944.

▲ Women in the midst of a gas smoke attack at their predictor and range finder in June 1942. ATS recruits on gun sites have to take weekly gas drills under smoke and tear gas.

◄ Women of the ATS who repaired army vehicles at a Royal Electrical and Mechanical Engineers (REME) workshop in 1944.

2

WOMEN'S AUXILIARY AIR FORCE (WAAF)

The women of the WAAF were charged with keeping the men flying. As with the other auxiliary services, initially they undertook domestic duties to release men for duty. However, within three years they were working as mechanics, electricians, engineers and fitters to literally keep the RAF in the air.

The British used radar to detect and track aircraft up to 200 miles away, giving the RAF a major strategic advantage. The WAAF were employed in the vital roles of operating the radar and plotting information in real time. If an aircraft crashed at sea, the data plotted by the WAAF radar team was essential to locating and rescuing the air crew.

The WAAF also operated over 1,000 barrage balloon sites, which was physically demanding, as they had to raise and lower balloons measuring over 20m in length and 9m in height. The balloons were designed as deterrents to enemy aircraft.

▲ In June 1941, recruits put aside high heels and are issued with comfortable-fitting shoes – without coupons. The comfort of these shoes is proved by the smart marching of the WAAF.

◄ Members of the WAAF take morning physical training amongst the spring flowers, May 1941.

▲ To free up men to fight at the front, women are seen here attending the WAAF School of Accountants, Wales, December 1942.

▲ WAAF policewomen go through thorough training in police work before they are posted out for patrol work, which is mainly for welfare work among servicewomen. They go through a course of unarmed combat, just in case anyone wants to get rough; taking evidence, street accidents and first-aid duties are part of the course. Here, first aid and taking of evidence in street-accident cases training is shown, January 1942.

▲ WAAF mechanics lying on the tail of a Hurricane fighter, June 1943.

▲ WAAF personnel dealing with the freight on its arrival at a Transport Command station, which deals with traffic overseas. This is a new command of the RAF in November 1943.

▲ A WAAF driver discusses the arming of a bomber with its crew.

➤ Two members of the WAAF had a fight on their hands with an errant barrage balloon in May 1941. When women were drafted into the WAAF as a means of freeing up men to fight for the RAF, most of their duties were on the ground, but they weren't 'soft' jobs. They were mainly employed to help maintain Britain's air defences, such as barrage balloons or AA guns.

WOMEN OF THE HOME FRONT

◄ A WAAF radar operator plotting aircraft on the cathode ray tube monitor, August 1945.

On the board in the image:

DATE: 15th SEPT., 1940
TIME: 11·00 HOURS
MAIN RAID
H 0-109
150 Aircraft

▲ Lord Dowding revisits the Battle of Britain operations room. Air Chief Marshal Lord Dowding in the operations room of No. 11 Group RAF Fighter Command Uxbridge, which was fully manned and operating for the last time. During the war, this was one of the 'nerve centres' of the Battle of Britain. The historic days were being relived when this picture was taken during a return peacetime visit by Air Chief Marshal Lord Dowding in April 1958, who was head of Fighter Command during the battle.

▲ It looks as though these WAAFs are trying to make the top of the tall chimney their 'target'. They are seen here loading hundreds of thousands of salvaged aluminium milk-bottle caps into lorries in the Midland County Dairy yard, Birmingham, to help to build more aeroplanes, March 1943.

➤ These four women of the WAAF are working on the Rolls-Royce engine of a Hurricane, July 1942.

▲ WAAFs on an RAF base wheel out their bicycles at the end of their shifts in 1942. They were issued with bikes to save fuel.

▲ Women of the WAAF with a theodolite and balloon for meterological observation at an RAF bomber station, 25 September 1942.

▲ WAAFs at the photography school learning to set out an aerial mosaic, April 1944.

➤ 'Annie get your gun.' A WAAF armourer loaded down with ammunition prior to it being put on board a bomber, September 1942.

WOMEN OF THE HOME FRONT

▲ A WAAF flight mechanic with a parachute before a test flight at Trainer Station, South Cerney, Wiltshire, on 14 October 1942.

⋏ A WAAF with a couple of Browning machine guns perched on her shoulders.

◀ WAAF and RAF ground crew roller-skating at their station, June 1942. A Westland Lysander communication aircraft can be seen in the background.

▲ The women are loosening up for the new season in July 1944. They are members of the Fairey Aircraft women's football section, and are training for matches to be arranged with WAAF and ATS women whose teams they hope to trounce on their home aerodromes and gun sites in Manchester.

▲ Women of the WAAF enjoying the sunshine after being patients as the hospital, September 1941.

▲ Volunteers of the Women's Air Training Corps attend a church parade at Christ Church on Princess Road, Manchester. Colonel J. Murray of the Army Cadets Force takes the salute at the march past in June 1944.

▲ Six hundred Polish women arrived in the UK from Russia, Persia and Africa after escaping from Poland to join the WAAF. Many had harrowing tales to tell and many had fathers and husbands to find in the UK or serving with Polish forces. Few could speak English. Here, in April 1944, a chalkboard with English and Polish instructions and a model are used to help the women understand elementary commands such as turning. Despite being in the country such a short time they picked up their life in the WAAF quickly.

▲ WAAF band on parade, September 1942.

JANE
ON THE LAND

JAN
FLAGS
DOW

◄ These cartoons, entitled 'Jane' or the 'Diary of a Bright Young Thing', appeared in *The Mirror* six days a week and depicted a series of mishaps that resulted in Jane's clothes being ripped or torn off for totally innocent reasons. Its popularity peaked during the Second World War, when Prime Minister Winston Churchill labelled Jane the British war effort's secret weapon. Actress Chrystabel Leighton Porter modelled for Jane.

3

WOMEN'S LAND ARMY (WLA)

For women from urban areas, the outdoor lifestyle of the WLA may have been very appealing. Yet for many, the reality was living in basic conditions on a remote farm. It was hard work, toiling 48–50 hours a week, and life could be lonely, but towards the end of the war, increasing numbers of land girls lived together in hostels rather than on site.

The land girls took on a huge variety of jobs, from milking cows, ploughing fields and harvesting crops to working as pest controllers. Britain was isolated during the war and had to grow its own food, so anything that could spoil crops was a serious threat. The land girls applied pesticides (made up of harmful chemicals) and they also had to catch rats. Not only did they lay the bait, but they also had the dubious task of clearing away the dead rats afterwards.

▲ Women's Land Army girls, probably on a farm in north Somerset in around June 1942.

▲ Harvesting oats in August 1941.

▲ Women's Land Army girls of all ages at work in the British countryside, 1944.

▲ 'Lending a hand on the land' at the Blunham, Bedfordshire, volunteer agricultural camp, where war workers and students are spending their Easter holidays helping on the land. Peggy Hopkins of Catford is tossed on a blanket for being late to the fields in the morning, 8 April 1944.

◄ On 9 August 1943, land girls are pulling down branches of hops that are infected with mildew as the special tractor goes down the line of hops spraying them with a wash to protect them before the gathering in September.

▲   Women of the WLA sowing potatoes on a farm in Essex with a new machine on
20 April 1942. The machine sows four rows of potatoes and covers them, doing the work of
eight people and a horse.

➤   Agriculture engineer and contractor R.H. Crawford of Frithville, Lincolnshire, bought
a battle-scarred ex-Alamein Sherman tank to pep up his agricultural contracts. This huge
tank, powered by coupled 90hp diesel engines, was to fight again – this time in the
all-important fight for the nation's bread. Women of the WLA at Carrington, who were
invited to the first trials, thoroughly enjoyed their first ride on the Sherman, but were also
keenly interested in the experiment. The Sherman ploughed 16 x 12in farrows.

▲ Sowing seed by broadcast method – scattering over a large area – on a farm in north Hampshire.

▲ The bride and groom, Horace Petts of the Auxiliary Fire Service (AFS) and Irene Punnett of the WLA, are carried from St Stephen's Church, Canterbury, on the shoulders of their colleagues after being wed.

➤ Gathering potatoes in a field – typically a man's job – in 1941.

▲ Recruits of the WLA prepare for ploughing at Hanley Brook, Upton-upon-Severn, Worcestershire, on 11 September 1942.

▲ American soldiers, getting ready to remove 4,000lb bombs, chat to land girls in the English countryside on 19 February 1944.

▲ In September 1943, 600 Oxfordshire land girls gave demonstrations of the latest methods of farming and food production, and held competitions in the grounds of Blenheim Palace. This happy band wagon collected for the Land Army Benevolent Fund.

▲ Women of the Forestry Commission section of the WLA at work.

▲ 20-year-old Lewis Betty and Peggy Clarke of Gateshead cutting logs in a Manchester timber farm, June 1945.

▲ They're warriors alright, but not the kind who used to march out of the old castle in the background – Maesllwch, Radnorshire – one of England's finest old strongholds, now a hostel for Land Army girls, c. 1940.

◄ A land girl in Sussex sitting on top of her Hitler snowman on 14 January 1942.

➤ Alison Jellicoe, 25-year-old member of the famous naval family, has by sheer hard work and the help of six land girls, turned the derelict Prune Farm, Underwood, Buckinghamshire, into a cattle-raising farm. Looking windswept, Jellicoe (left) and a colleague look out for stray lambs in April 1943.

Land girls on horseback in the British countryside in 1943.

▲ Recruits of the Women's Land Army (Pests Department) are employed in South Wales as rat catchers, and here show a record catch, March 1944.

▲ Miss Williams gives a pill through a tube to a sheep, August 1941.

▲ Giving a Jersey calf a brush down at Blackalls Farm in Cholsey, Berkshire, at the end of the war.

◀ At work feeding pigs on a farm in England around August 1941.

◄◄ Women of the WLA making a cup of tea on their break, March 1943.

◄ Victory Parade, 1946: land girls detachment.

WOMEN'S LAND ARMY (WLA) 95

4

WOMEN'S ROYAL NAVAL SERVICE (WRNS)

Vera Laughton Matthews had been an officer in the WRNS during the First World War and was appointed director of the new organisation in 1939. During the inter-war period she had become a champion of the Sea Ranger programme. The scheme enrolled girls aged 15–21 from seafaring communities or those who lived near water and were keen sailors. It was similar to Girl Guides and the rangers earned badges, learning how to crew boats and read nautical charts. With the onset of war, the Sea Rangers were keen to the join the WRNS when they were old enough.

Of the three auxiliary services, the WRNS was the smallest and therefore the most difficult to get into. The entry requirements were strict: a medical, a high standard of physical fitness – which had to be maintained during service – and a two-week probation period. In 1944 the number of officers and ratings peaked at 74,000.

▲ Young Wren cadets on a day out, 1945.

▲ Young girls of the sea scouts seen here keeping fit so they may join the Wrens, August 1943.

▲ The Sea Rangers combine land work with sea training at the camp at Cobham. They have been fruit picking and doing other land work as part of their training, October 1943.

▲ Wren PO (Petty Officer) Jillian Jenkinson taking rifle-training instruction from Instructor PO T. Didot at HMS *Wellesley*, North Western Gunnery Training Establishment, in April 1944.

▲ Sea Rangers at Cobham taking a well-deserved break in October 1943.

◄ Wrens marching to St Nicholas' Cathedral, Newcastle, for the navy and merchant navy thanksgiving service on 20 July 1942.

▲ In December 1941 it was decided that women in the UK between the ages of 20 and 30 should be called up for military service. Initially this meant manning AA guns like this one or doing so-called 'desk jobs' in order to free up men who had no other impediment to a military career.

▲ This Wren's job is to keep over 200 warships in order, March 1943. These models of warships belonging to all the nations of the war were used for instructing Fleet Air Arm fighter pilots in aerial recognition on board HMS *Heron*.

▲ Navy women get a taste of what life on board ship would be like, March 1941.

▲ Royal women were no exception to the plea to women to join in with the war effort; in fact their willingness to take work on encouraged other women to do so. Here is the Duchess of Kent in uniform, who joined the Wrens alongside her relative, Princess Elizabeth, later Queen Elizabeth II.

▲ An American sailor chatting to a Wren in a pub in Northern Ireland.

▲ Wrens on the River Tees, 16 February 1945.

◄ A Wren armourer cleaning an AA gun at a Royal Naval Air Station in England, September 1942.

▲ Wrens attached to the Fleet Air Arm, wearing pilots' uniform, placing a wireless in a Westland Lysander in September 1942. These were the first Wrens to fly.

▲ A bride and groom, Lieutenant Charles Henry Pearn and Wren Eilen Bennett, disturb geese on the village green at Sampford Spiney, south Dartmoor, October 1944.

▲ Wrens being fitted with demob clothes at the end of the war.

▲ Wrens, sailors and soldiers dance in the street in Brighton on VE Day.

5

WOMEN'S WAR WORK

As men joined the military, women took on their jobs and at the same time new roles opened up in industry to meet the demands of war. In general, the women received between half to two-thirds of the men's pay for doing the same jobs. Trade unions advocated lower wages for women in order to protect the interests of men when they returned from war. Unhappy with unequal pay, the women organised local strikes and demonstrations outside Parliament but with limited success.

Enemy bombing raids throughout the war put huge pressure on Britain's emergency services. Women were permitted to join the Auxiliary Fire Service (AFS) from 1938. They worked in the canteens, as drivers, dispatch riders and in the communication centres co-ordinating the deployment of fire crews. Although the actual fire-fighting and the most senior roles were reserved for men, by March 1943 32,200 women were serving full time in the fire service and 54,600 part time.

∧ A girl in a saw mill, July 1941.

▲ Women assembling cylinder studs on crank cases of Rolls-Royce Merlin engines at a factory in north-west England on 2 March 1942. Merlin engines were used in many RAF bombers and fighter aircraft.

▲ Workers at the Royal Ordnance factory at Chorley, Lancashire, destroy shells at the end of the war. The cordite is removed from 6-pounder shell cases.

▲ A record output of 200,000 bricks in forty-eight hours was reached by Blythe and Sons, Birtley. The staff, which included eight women and two ex-soldiers who were at Dunkirk, were working as never before in order to do their bit.

A These wives and mothers have banded themselves into an Aircraft Component Inspection Department and their 'factory' is in an off-licence somewhere in London. They work from 9 a.m. to 5 p.m. and rush home at midday to see to their children. Many thousands of parts pass through their hands every week.

➤ A woman delivers boxes full of fish to traders in Billingsgate market, London, 10 September 1943.

▲ Volunteer messengers take an active part in the working of the AFS, Birmingham, 6 September 1939.

▲ Fisherwomen of New Biggin hauling their boats ashore.

▲ Inspecting their catch.

▲ Keeping the kids out of mischief in a very hands-on way. The baby is kept an eye on as it is tied to the tree, while the group of women continue hop-picking in the fields of Kent, September 1941.

▲ Nurses giving Tube shelterers garlic oil for prevention of flu as they take cover at St Johns Wood Tube station during the Blitz.

◄ A St Johns nurse at work at the Villa Day Nursery, opened for the express purpose of releasing women for war work.

▲ Nurses take a record of the remains in the midst of the bomb damage at London Hospital, 7 July 1944.

➤ Odeon usherettes looking for ladders in a new kind of hose – and not the silk kind – in February 1943. They form a fire-fighting squad at the cinema in Leicester Square and have had a lot of experience during the Blitz.

◄ Conductresses ready for work – off to start their new careers, July 1940.

▲ Joan Garside of Prestwick, a former stage acrobat and trapeze artist, was one of the first women tram drivers.

▲ A woman in a Ministry of Supply munitions depot works on the caterpillar track of a tank in 1941.

⌃ A railway inspector and women cleaners working on an engine in the floodlit pit of a train shed, 1944.

❯ The first women railway porters on duty at Crewe station, 1942.

◄ Girls strike outside the Houses of Parliament in London in September 1942.

▲ A deputation of women war workers seen here in Whitehall following a meeting over minimum wages, September 1942.

➤ Women working on the stern of a vessel in October 1944.

◄ Women dockers at a northern port. Mrs Hunter (with load on back), mother of four children and whose husband is in the forces, photographed at work on the docks in November 1941.

▲ Plymouth's team of women navvies completing their Blitz-time ambition on 7 August 1947: working alone as a team without male supervision, they have brought the house down unaided. They loved the work and would continue as an all-women gang in the future.

▲ High up on a tottering wall, Lydia Walker steps across the gap aided by Betty Baker. Both are working with the two teams of women clearing up the ruins of Plymouth.

▲ 'For men must work and women must sweep' might be the slogan of Ada Riches, of Woodbridge, Suffolk. She had always swept her own chimneys, but took on the job for Woodbridge and the surrounding villages during the war. Riches took her brushes, rods and sootbag around on a bicycle. The head and hair protector, reminiscent of the middle ages, was her own design.